Christmas

MADE EASY

Crafts

Publications International, Ltd.

Products used in *Christmas Crafts Made Easy:* (Available in most arts and crafts stores.)

Creamcoat by Delta Artist's Acrylic Paints (Jolly Santa Post. Well-Lit Welcome)

Black & Decker Two-Temperature Glue Gun (Jolly Santa Post)

DMC Embroidery Floss (Stitched Yule Accessories, Christmas Cheer Mugs)

Kreinik Blager Heavy Braid (Stitched Yule Accessories, Lacy Angel Vest)

Velcro Hook and Loop Tape (Stitched Yule Accessories)

Maxwell International, black fabric cord (Stitched Yule Accessories)

Fond Memories, acrylic coasters (Yuletide Coasters)

Daniel Enterprises, red mugs (Christmas Cheer Mugs)

Liquitex Concentrated Artists Colors Yellow Light and Laquer Red (Poinsettia Place Settings)

Deka Permanent Fabric Paint Medium Green (Poinsettia Place Settings)

DecoArt Fabric Acrylic Paints Heavy Metals Light (Diamond Yellow, Sparkling Ruby), Shimmering Pearls (Lime Green) (Poinsettia Place Settings)

Tulip Paint Writer (Yellow) (Poinsettia Place Settings) Colorpoint and Glitter Fabric Paint (Gingerbread Tree Skirt)

Majestic Bendable Ribbon (Poinsettia Place Settings)

Sculpey Colored Modeling Compound (Family Fun Project)

Therm O Web, Inc. HeatnBond Original No-Sew adhesive (Lacy Angel Vest, Satin Wreath Sweatshirt, Gingerbread Tree Skirt)

Marvy Fabric Marker (Lacy Angel Vest)

THE BEADERY Craft Products Rhinestones, faceted stones, stars, cabochons, pony beads (Lacy Angel Vest, Snowman Stocking)

Aleene's OK To Wash-It Fabric Glue (Lacy Angel Vest)

Jones Tones Aurora Flakes and Aurora Dust Dimensional Glitter; Stretch Fabric Paint: Enamels—Green, Red, Black; Liquid Foil Pearl; Glitter Copper (Peek-A-Boo T-Shirt, Gingerbread Tree Skirt)

Craft Designers: Beth Franks pages (30, 34, 40, 98), Bev George (pages 68, 94, 108), Joan Green (pages 26, 78, 82, 102), Kathy Lamancusa (pages 44, 54, 72, 86, 90), Delores Ruzicka (pages 58, 62), The Beadery (page 50)

Contributing Writers: Betty Valle, Delores Ruzicka

Technical Advisor: Melissa Birdsong

Photography: Sacco Productions Limited/Chicago

Photographers: Tom O'Connell, Peter Ross

Photo Stylist: Diane Pronites

Models: Karen Blaschek, Sherrie Withers, Ashley Pincus/Royal Model Management

Contents

Introduction

Christmastide is the happiest time of the year for children and adults alike! But time always seems at a premium—especially during the holidays. Crafting at Christmas is a wonderful way to escape the crowded shopping malls and the mad race to find that "perfect" gift. This is also the time when creating decorations and presents is most fun and fulfilling—and appreciated by those receiving lovingly handcrafted gifts. With *Christmas Crafts Made Easy*, you'll be able to make something wonderful for just about everyone on your gift list right at home—and they can all be made in less than a day!

The projects in this book include a wide variety of techniques and methods. Take a moment and look through the pages. You'll find everything from traditional counted cross-stitch to appliqué. Each project has complete step-by-step instructions and photos to help

make everything easy to understand and fun to do. And remember, things made by hand come from the heart.

We hope you enjoy creating these projects. They are for all skill levels and interests, and you'll find that many of the projects use basic items you already have around your home. Once you begin, you'll see that creating your own gifts and holiday decorations is a satisfying and relaxing way to get ready for the holidays.

What You'll Find

JEWELRY MAKING

Although the jewelry in this book looks sophisticated, most is made by gluing. *Jewelry findings* is a term for a variety of

ready-made metal components used as attachments and fastenings to assemble jewelry. They are usually made of inexpensive metal. Findings include pin backs, earring parts, barrel clasps, jump rings, and beading

wire. For our projects you will need a pin back and earring findings. All of these items are easily found in your local craft or hobby store.

POLYMER CLAY

There are several polymer clays on the market. All are intermixable and offer you endless options for creating different objects. The clays are quite hard when first unwrapped and must be kneaded until soft and pliable. Make sure not to use the clay before it reaches this stage—if you do, you may cause air pockets that will crack as the clay is manipulated. This can cause the clay to break apart. After you have worked your clay until it is soft, roll it into logs. You can proceed with your project at this point.

When you have finished forming your clay object, you will need to bake it to harden it.

Follow the instructions on the package for baking times and temperatures—baking at the right time and temperature may take some practice. If you don't bake the clay long enough, it becomes crumbly, but if you bake it too long it may burn. When the clay comes out of the oven, it will be a bit soft; it hardens as it cools. It is best to bake the clay objects on a nonconducting surface, such as thick, tempered glass (Pyrex®); slate; or a ceramic pan.

Caution: Do not bake above 265 degrees Fahrenheit, and use a separate thermometer to verify actual oven temperature. Do not overbake, as fumes may be toxic. If the baking time is lengthened, lower the temperature to 250 degrees Fahrenheit. Do not ingest polymer clay, and supervise children at all times when baking.

CROSS-STITCH

Cross-stitch is traditionally worked on an "even-weave" cloth that has vertical and horizontal threads of equal thickness and spacing. Six-strand embroidery floss is used for most stitching; there are also many beautiful threads that can be used to enhance the appearance of the stitching. Finishing and framing a counted cross-stitch piece will complete your work. There are many options in framing—just visit your local craft shop or framing gallery.

Basic Supplies
Fabric: The most common even-weave fabric is 14-count Aida

cloth. The weave of this fabric creates distinct squares that make stitching very easy for the beginner.

Needles, Hoops, and Scissors: A blunt-end or tapestry needle is used for counted cross-stitch. A #24 needle is the recommended size for stitching on 14-count Aida cloth. You may use an embroidery hoop while stitching—just be sure to remove it when not working on your project. A small pair of sharp scissors are a definite help when working with embroidery floss.

Floss: Six-strand cotton embroidery floss is most commonly used, and it's usually cut into 18-inch lengths for stitching. Use two of the six strands for stitching on 14-count Aida cloth. Also use two strands for backstitching.

Preparing to Stitch

The materials list will tell you what size cloth to use. To locate the center of the design, lightly fold your fabric in half and in half again. Find the center of the chart by following the arrows on the sides.

Reading the chart is easy, since each square on the chart equals one stitch on the fabric. The colors correspond to the floss numbers listed in the color key. Select a color and stitch all of that color within an area. Begin by holding the thread ends behind the fabric until secured or covered over with two or three stitches. You may skip a few stitches on the back of the material, but do not run the thread from one area to another behind a section that will not be stitched in the finished piece—it will show through the fabric. If your thread begins to twist, drop the needle and allow the thread to untwist. It is important to the final appearance of the project to keep an even tension when pulling stitches through so that all stitches will have a uniform look. To end a thread, weave or run the thread under several stitches on the back side. Cut the ends close to the fabric.

Each counted cross-stitch is represented by a colored square on the project's chart. For horizontal rows, work the stitches in two steps, i.e., all of the left to right stitches and then all of the right to left stitches (see Figure A). For vertical rows, work each complete stitch as shown in Figure B. Three-quar-ter stitches are often used when the design requires two colors in one square or to allow more detail in the pattern (See Figure C) The backstitch is often used to outline or create letters, and is shown by bold lines on the patterns. Backstitch is usually worked after the pattern is completed (See Figure D).

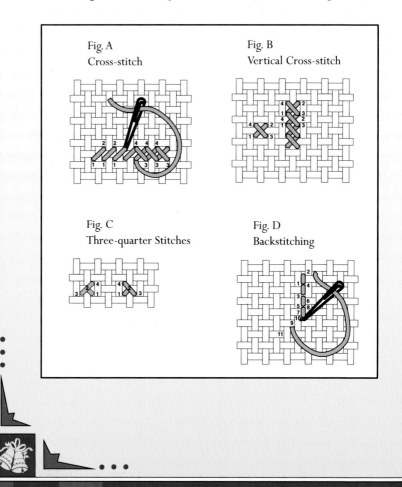

Fig. A
Cross-stitch

Fig. B
Vertical Cross-stitch

Fig. C
Three-quarter Stitches

Fig. D
Backstitching

PLASTIC CANVAS

Plastic canvas allows for three-dimensional stitchery projects.

Basic Supplies

Plastic Canvas: Canvas is most widely available by the sheet. Stitch all the pieces of a project on the same brand of plastic canvas to ensure that the meshes will match.

Plastic canvas comes in several counts or mesh sizes (number

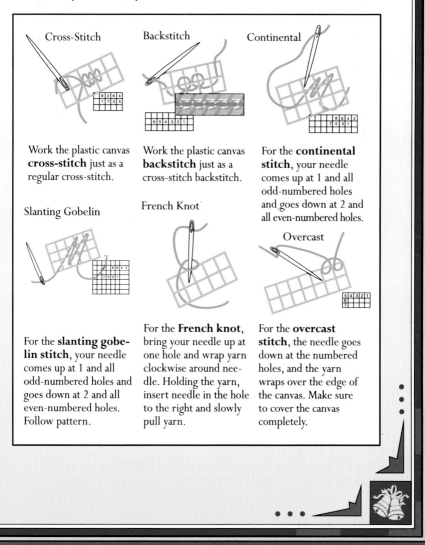

Cross-Stitch

Work the plastic canvas **cross-stitch** just as a regular cross-stitch.

Backstitch

Work the plastic canvas **backstitch** just as a cross-stitch backstitch.

Continental

For the **continental stitch,** your needle comes up at 1 and all odd-numbered holes and goes down at 2 and all even-numbered holes.

Slanting Gobelin

For the **slanting gobelin stitch**, your needle comes up at 1 and all odd-numbered holes and goes down at 2 and all even-numbered holes. Follow pattern.

French Knot

For the **French knot,** bring your needle up at one hole and wrap yarn clockwise around needle. Holding the yarn, insert needle in the hole to the right and slowly pull yarn.

Overcast

For the **overcast stitch,** the needle goes down at the numbered holes, and the yarn wraps over the edge of the canvas. Make sure to cover the canvas completely.

of stitches to the inch) and numerous sizes of sheets.

Specialty sizes and shapes such as circles are also available. Most canvas is clear, although up to 24 colors are available. Colored canvas is used when parts of the project remain unstitched. Seven-count canvas comes in four weights—standard; a thinner, flexible weight; a stiffer, rigid weight; and a softer weight made especially for bending and curved projects. Designs can be stitched on any mesh count—the resulting size of the project is the only thing that will be affected. The smaller the count number, the larger the project will be, since the count number refers to the number of stitches per inch. Therefore, 7-count canvas has seven stitches per inch, while 14-count has 14. A 14-count project will be half the size of a 7-count project if two identical projects were stitched on 7-count and 14-count canvas.

Needles: Needle size is determined by the count size of the plastic canvas you are using. Patterns generally call for a #18 needle for stitching on 7-count plastic canvas, a #16 or #18 for 10-count canvas, and a #22 or #24 for stitching on 14-count plastic canvas.

Yarns: A wide variety of yarns may be used. The most common is worsted weight (or 4-

ply). Acrylic yarns are less expensive and washable; wool may also be used. Several companies produce specialty yarns for plastic canvas work. These cover the canvas well and will not "pill" as some acrylics do. Sport-weight yarn (or 3-ply) and embroidery floss are often used on 10-count canvas. Use 12 strands or double the floss thickness for 10-count canvas and 6 strands for stitching on 14-count canvas. On 14-count plastic canvas, many of the specialty metallic threads made for cross-stitch can be used to highlight and enhance your project.

Cutting Out Your Project

Many plastic canvas projects are dimensional—a shape has to be cut out and stitched. Scissors or a craft knife are recommended.

Preparing to Stitch

Cut your yarn to a 36-inch length. Begin by holding the yarn end behind the fabric until secured or covered over with two or three stitches. To end a length, weave or run the yarn under several stitches on the back side. Cut the end close to the canvas. The continental stitch is the most commonly used stitch to cover plastic canvas. Decorative stitches will add interest and texture to your project. As in cross-stitch, if your yarn begins to twist, drop the needle and allow the yarn to untwist. It is important to the final appearance of the project to keep an even tension when pulling your stitches through so that all of your stitches have a uniform look. Do not pull your stitches too tight, since this causes gaps in your stitching and allows the canvas to show through between your stitches. Also, do not carry one color yarn across several rows of another color on the back—the carried color may show through to the front of your project. Do not stitch the outer edge of the canvas until the other stitching is complete. If the project is a single piece of canvas, overcast the outer edge with the color specified. If there are two or more pieces, follow the pattern instructions for assembly.

Cleaning

If projects are stitched with acrylic yarn, they may be washed by hand using warm or cool water and a mild detergent. Place on a terry cloth towel to air dry. Do not place in a dryer or dry clean.

WEARABLES

You'll find fabric painting to be fast, easy, and fun. With the latest developments in fabric paints, using basic dimensional paints is almost as easy as writing with a ballpoint pen. Some of the painting projects will require a brush—we'll tell you what type of brush you'll need in the project's materials list.

Using a Shirt Board

You might want a commercially purchased shirt board, or you can make your own by cutting corrugated cardboard into the shape of a flattened T-shirt about ½ inch smaller than the shirt you'll be using. Cover it with wax paper and insert it into the item you'll be working on—it will prevent paint from bleeding through, and it will make it easier for you to transport a project with wet paint. Make sure the waxed side is under the surface you want to paint.

Paints: Each of the projects will specify the type of paints required. Only dimensional and embellished paints, which are especially formulated to use on fabric, are used. For specific instructions for each paint, follow the instructions on the packaging or bottle.

Basic Guidelines for Wearables

1. Prewash garments without using any softeners. Softeners prevent the paint from bonding completely with the fibers. Press out any wrinkles.

2. If you're right-handed, work on your project from the upper left-hand corner to the lower right-hand corner (and vice-versa for left-handers). Paint all colors as you go. This will prevent you from accidentally smearing the paint with your elbow or hand.

3. When using dimensional paints, pick up the tube of paint with the cap on and shake the paint down into the tip to remove any air bubbles each time you use a color. Place a paint bottle down on its side between uses.

4. Hold your dimensional paint bottle like a ball-point pen. Squeeze gently to push out paint. Work quickly and smoothly. Moving too slowly often results in a "bumpy" appearance.

5. When using dimensional glitter paint, be sure to draw a line of paint that is thick enough to carry the glitter.

6. Allow paints to dry at least 6 to 8 hours before touching. Allow 36 to 48 hours for paint to be completely cured before wearing.

Caring for Your Wearable

Hand or machine wash in lukewarm water—NOT COLD!!—in delicate/knit cycle. Cold water will crack the paint. Tumble dry on low for a few minutes to remove wrinkles, then remove and lay flat to dry. Do not wash in Woolite or other delicate care products.

Sewing

The excitement of making your own holiday crafts sometimes gets in the way of your preparation. Before plunging into your chosen project, check to make sure you have all the materials needed. Being prepared will make your sewing easier and more fun. Most of the items you need will probably be on hand already.

Scissors: Two styles are needed, one about eight to ten inches long with bent handles for cutting fabric. This style of scissors allows you to cut through fabric while it lays flat. These shears should be sharp and used only for fabric. The second style of scissors is smaller, about six inches, with sharp points. You will need this style for smaller projects and close areas.

Straight Pins: Nonrusting dressmaker pins are best. They will not leave rust marks on your fabric if they come in contact with dampness or glue. And dressmaker's pins have very sharp points for easy insertion.

Tape Measure: A plastic-coated tape measure is recommended because it will not stretch and may be wiped clean if it comes in contact with paint or glue.

Ironing Board and Steam Iron: Be sure your ironing board is well padded and has a clean covering. Sometimes you do more sewing with the iron than you do with the sewing machine. Keeping your fabrics, seams, and hems pressed cuts down on stitches and valuable

time. A steam or dry iron is best. It is important to press your fabric to achieve a professional look. The iron is also used to adhere fusible adhesive. Keep the bottom of your iron clean and free of any substance that could mark your fabric. The steam iron may be used directly on most fabrics with no shine. Test a small piece of the fabric first. If it causes a shine on the right side, try the reverse side.

Thread: Have mercerized sewing thread in the colors needed for each project you have chosen. Proper shade and strength (about a 50 weight) of thread avoids having the stitching show more than is necessary and lends the item a finished look.

Fusible Adhesive: Fusible adhesive is placed paper-side up on the wrong side of your material. Place the iron on the paper side of the adhesive and press for one to three seconds. Allow the fabric to cool. The design can then be drawn or traced onto the paper side and cut out. Remove the paper and place the material right-side up in the desired position on your project and iron for three to five seconds.

Sewing Machine: Neat, even stitches are achieved in a very few minutes with a sewing machine. If desired, you may machine-stitch a zigzag stitch around the attached fusible adhesive pieces to secure the edges.

Work Surface: Your sewing surface should be a comfortable height for sitting and roomy enough to lay out your projects. Keep it clean and free of other crafting materials that could accidentally spill or soil your fabric.

THE BAND SAW

The band saw is a very handy, easy-to-use tool for the home workshop. It may be easily operated by a man, woman, or an older child with supervision. A band saw may sit on your workbench or it may also have its own legs or stand. Band saws do not take up much space.

Respect your band saw—Safety First! Before you begin to saw, read your instruction manual. Always keep in mind these simple safety hints:
Keep your work area clean and uncluttered.
Don't use the band saw in damp or wet locations.
Keep your work area well-lit.
Do not force the band saw to saw through items that it is not designed for.
Wear proper clothing—nothing loose or baggy.
Wear safety goggles.
Never leave the band saw running unattended.

One advantage of the band saw is its versatility. The fast cutting saw uses a flexible steel blade, in the form of a continuous loop, that runs over two rubber wheels. To use the saw, feed the wood into the blade. For straight, fast cutting, use a wide, coarse-toothed blade; for curve cutting, use a narrower blade. Don't try to turn corners that are too tight for the blade width; if you do the blade will burn and the wood may become wedged onto the sawblade. The $3/26$-inch blade will cut a one-inch circle, the $1/2$-inch blade will cut a 2 $1/2$-inch circle, and the $3/4$-inch blade will cut a 3 $1/2$-inch circle.

When operating the saw, set the upper blade guide about $1/4$ to $1/2$ inch above the work. Band saw blades are reasonably priced and stay sharp a long time. It is practical to throw away the old ones rather than to sharpen them. Never use a dull blade!

Most band saws are equipped with a tilting table for beveling and for cutting objects at an angle. Sometimes it is necessary to turn the work upside down to make certain parts of a cut. After practicing with your band saw, you will become more comfortable with it.

A WORD ABOUT GLUE

Glue can be a sticky subject when you don't use the right one for the job. There are many different glues on the craft market today, each formulated for a different crafting purpose.

The following are ones you should be familiar with:

White Glue: This may be used as an all-purpose glue—it dries clear and flexible. It is often referred to as craft glue or tacky glue. Tacky on contact, it allows you to put two items together without a lot of set-up time required. It is used for most projects, especially ones involving wood, plastics, some fabrics, and cardboard.

Thin-Bodied Glues: Use these glues when your project requires a smooth, thin layer of glue. Thin-bodied glues work well on some fabrics and papers.

Fabric Glue: This type of glue is made to bond with fabric fibers and withstand repeated washing. Use this kind of glue for attaching rhinestones and/or other charms to fabric projects. Some glues require heat-setting. Check the bottle for complete instructions.

Hot Melt Glue: Formed into cylindrical sticks, this glue is inserted into a hot-temperature glue gun and heated to maintain a liquid state. Depending on the type of glue gun used, the glue is forced out through the gun's nozzle by either pushing on the end of the glue stick or squeezing a trigger. Use clear glue sticks for projects using wood, fabrics, most plastics, ceramics, and cardboard. When using any glue gun, be careful of the noz-zle and the freshly applied glue—it is very hot! Apply glue to the piece being attached. Work with small areas at a time so that the glue doesn't set before being pressed into place.

Low Melt Glue: This is similar to hot melt glues in that it is formed into sticks and requires a glue gun to be used. Low melt glues are used for projects that would be damaged by heat. Examples include foam, balloons, and metallic ribbons. Low melt glue sticks are oval-shaped and can only be used in a low-temperature glue gun.

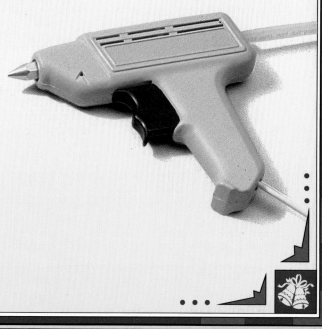

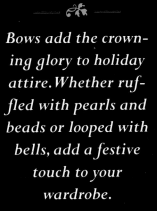

Bows add the crown-
ing glory to holiday
attire. Whether ruf-
fled with pearls and
beads or looped with
bells, add a festive
touch to your
wardrobe.

• MATERIALS •

Looped Barrette:

3¾ inch barrette

Spool wire

Wire cutters

1⅜ yards ribbon, 1½ inches wide

1 yard gathered ribbon

6 small jingle bells

Fabric glue

Ruffled Ribbon:

1 yard ribbon, 2½ inches wide

Needle and thread

44 pearl beads

20 plated beads

2¾ inch barrette

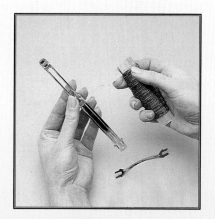

1 For looped barrette: Open barrette and remove spring by pinching and pulling at center. Set spring aside. Slip wire through hole in end of barrette and twist to secure. Wrap wire around barrette several times.

3 Pull up about 3 inches of ribbon and make a loop about 1½ inches tall. Pinch ribbon and wrap wire around ribbon and barrette several times to secure. Continue making loops and securing them to barrette with wire. You should be able to make approximately 12 loops and still have a 3-inch tail of ribbon at end of barrette.

2 Pinch ribbon about three inches from wired end. Place on barrette at wired end and wrap wire around ribbon and barrette several times to secure.

1 For ruffled ribbon:
Fold ribbon in half
lengthwise and make a faint
crease; follow crease as you
sew. Secure thread at one
end of ribbon in the center
using a double stitch. The
thread should be doubled
and knotted at end. Sew a
running stitch down crease.
Stitches should be approximately $\frac{1}{2}$ inch apart.

4 Slip wire through hole
at end of barrette and
twist to secure. Trim wire
end. Trim ribbon ends at an
angle. Replace spring in barrette. Cut gathered ribbon
into lengths, two each of $4\frac{1}{2}$
inches, 4 inches, and $3\frac{1}{2}$
inches. Glue bells at one end
of ribbons and glue other
ends between loops.

2 Hold ribbon in one hand and thread ends in other. Carefully pull thread in one direction and push ribbon in the other to create ruffle. When ruffle is desired length, tie or sew thread ends securely. Trim thread.

3 Cut off 16 inches of wire. Bend spool wire in half and twist a few times at end with the bend. Thread half the beads on one side of wire and half the beads on the other side in an alternating pattern—two pearl beads followed by one plated bead.

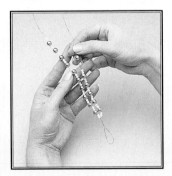

4 Twist wire at every other group of pearl beads to create a pattern as shown. Do not twist last group at either end of wire.

5 Place beaded wire lengthwise across top of the ruffle. Bring ends of wire around back of ruffle and twist them together securely. Trim any excess wire.

6 Glue barrette to back of ruffle.

A vest magically becomes a holiday in itself! Frosted with lace trim and a winsome angel and accented with sparkling jewels, all this was made with an iron and some paint!

• MATERIALS •

1 yard fusible webbing

½ yard scalloped border lace, with star motif

Iron

Wax paper

Man's vest

12 x 6 inches white washable satin

Brown fabric marker

Muslin scraps (3 × 6 inches)

15m ombre metallic thread

Fabric paint: ivory, gold glitter

20 crystal acrylic rhinestones, 7mm and 8mm

Fabric glue

1 Lay back side of lace on fusible adhesive; cover with wax paper.

Place medium iron on wax paper; press for three to five seconds, flip over and iron on paper side of adhesive and press for three seconds. Pull wax paper off lace while warm. Let cool. Pull lace off paper; cut into desired shapes (trim extra adhesive from lace when cutting shapes; it will melt into fabric). Leave four stars uncut for angel wings.

2 Iron adhesive to back of satin and muslin. Place iron on medium setting on paper side of adhesive, press for three to five seconds. Trace patterns on the paper back of prepared materials. Use white for two angel dresses and muslin for two head circles. Cut out and peel paper off appliqués.

3 Place scalloped border around neckline of vest and top of left pocket. Assemble angels, one on right side of vest and one on back. Position extra lace stars around vest. Iron to adhere pieces.

4 With marker, draw face on head following pattern. Make 14 loopy pom-pons by winding metallic thread around two fingers 12 times; tie off in center using a separate piece of thread. Glue seven pom-pons around each angel's head using fabric glue.

5 Outline lace and stars with gold fabric paint and angel with ivory fabric paint (rest tip on edge to steady line). Add ivory dots to make extra fill-in stars. Glue rhinestones to vest with fabric glue.

✱ See page 114 for pattern

A plastic canvas belt, brooch, and earrings add sparkle to even the plainest outfit. Make a striking fashion statement!

• M A T E R I A L S •

Belt:

⅓ sheet clear plastic canvas, #10 mesh

Tapestry needles, #20 and #24

4 skeins black embroidery floss

Metallic thread, 1 spool each; red, green, gold

49 gold beads, 3mm each

1½ inches hook and loop tape, ⅝ inches

Black sewing thread and needle

6mm presewn black fabric cord, double waist size plus 6 inches

Brooch and Earrings:

⅙ sheet plastic canvas, #10 mesh

Metallic thread, 5 yards gold, 3 yards green, 2 yards red

15 gold beads, 3mm each

1 bar pin

1 set pierced earring findings (post-type)

Glue gun

Belt Instructions:

Cut plastic canvas 69 holes × 36 holes. Trim according to pattern lines.

Use small manicure scissors or craft knife to trim shaded areas for slots for cording.

Stitching: Using #20 needle, work metallic portions of design in continental stitch. Fill in the background in continental stitch using black floss. To stitch with floss, cut a 2-yard length of floss, double it (making 12 strands), and thread cut ends through needle. Bring needle through canvas, holding looped end on back side. Make first stitch and pass needle through loop on back. Draw thread firmly to secure floss to canvas. When finished stitching, overcast outer edge and inside slots using double strand of black.

Attach beads to belt using a double strand of sewing thread and #24 needle. Knot end of thread and weave into stitching on back. Bring needle to front at point marked on chart for bead placement, slip a bead on needle and insert needle back through the same hole. When all beads are attached, knot end of thread and weave in ends securely.

Cut fabric cord in half. Fold one piece of cord in half and attach to side of belt with lark's head knot (see picture) through slot. Place belt around waist and pin hook and loop tape strips. Pull fabric cord covering back ¾ inch and remove a small amount of core material. Turn fabric ends in and sew strips in

place, sewing through all layers to secure.

Brooch and Earrings Instructions:

Cut one piece canvas 23 holes × 23 holes and two pieces 11 holes × 15 holes. Trim according to pattern lines. Stitch the brooch and earrings entirely in continental stitch. Overcast all edges with gold. Attach beads according to belt instructions.

Use glue gun to attach bar pin to back of brooch. Glue earring posts to back of earrings.

✳See page 116 for pattern

Peek-A-Boo T-Shirt

MATERIALS

T-shirt

12-inch-square green
   Christmas material

Straight pins

Sewing machine

White thread

Pinking shears

Fabric paint: green, red

Fabric glitter

Craft knife

60 heart pony beads,
   assortment of solid and
   translucent red, two
   shades of green

Scissors

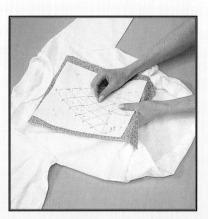

1 Copy and enlarge pattern on page 39. Turn T-shirt inside out (sewing is done on inside). Center Christmas fabric (right-side down) 1 inch from neck ribbing. Position paper tree pattern on top of material, and pin three layers (single layer of T-shirt, Christmas material, paper pattern) together. Use a lot of pins so fabrics won't shift and pleat.

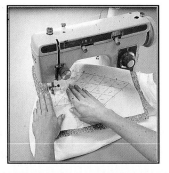

2 Machine stitch on top of pattern lines starting in bottom left corner: A (stitch to) > M > L > B > C > K > J > D > E > I > H > F > G. Now change angle but DON'T CUT THREAD, at bottom right corner G > M > N > F > E > O > P > D > C > Q > R > B > A. At bottom left corner DON'T CUT THREAD, A > S > V > U > T > V > U > S > G. Now cut thread.

3 Remove paper (paper is perforated due to stitch line); it will rip away. Trim excess Christmas fabric with pinking shears, within ½ inch of outside tree seam. Reverse shirt. Outline tree and trunk with fine line of green fabric paint. For ornaments, add small red dots at stitching intersections. Sprinkle wet paint with fabric glitter. Let dry. Shake off excess glitter. Don't wash shirt for 72 hours.

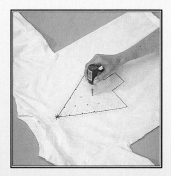

5 Fold up bottom of shirt four inches, with right sides together, and pin. Mark cutting lines about 2½ to 3 inches long and ¼ inch apart around shirt.

4 Using craft knife, make a small slit in center of stitched diamond (top layer only). Cut from center to each point, then cut each quarter flap in half again. This will give eight points to diamonds.

6 Cut on marked lines, through both layers of T-shirt. Cut three strips across fold, then skip one. Repeat around shirt. Remove pins.

7 Tie matching ends together with a double knot. To add color, string a bead on strip before tying. Cut remaining strips and tie.

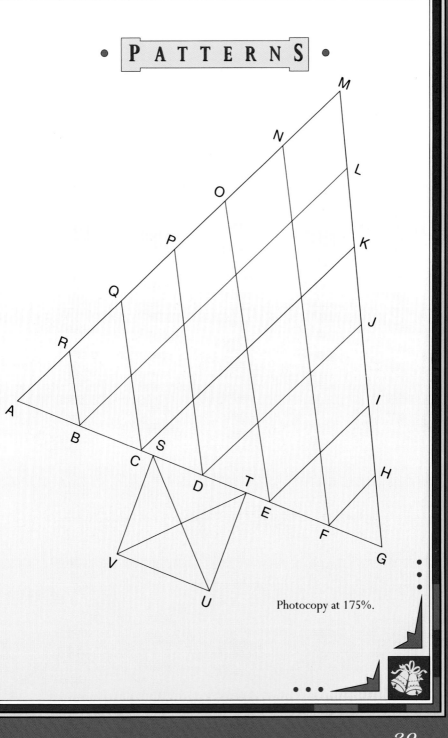

PATTERNS

Photocopy at 175%.

Who would have thought that a black sweatshirt could be so elegant—and so easy to make! With an iron and some paint, you can create your favorite and most comfortable holiday attire.

• M A T E R I A L S •

Black sweatshirt

Iron

Freezer paper

⅓ yard washable green satin

⅓ yard washable red satin

1 yard fusible adhesive

Fabric paint: red, green, gold glitter

1 Reverse sweatshirt. Iron wax side of freezer paper to inside of sweatshirt neckline (front and back). Turn sweatshirt right-side out.

2 Iron fusible adhesive to back of red and green satin. Place iron on medium setting and iron paper side of adhesive; press for three to five seconds. Trace patterns on the paper back of prepared satin. Use red for bow, bow knot, and bow ties, and five to eight berries. Use green for 13 to 16 small and 5 to 7 large holly leaves. Cut out and peel paper off appliqué pieces.

3 Place bow off-center, about ½ inch from neckline. Place bow ties below bow. Place holly leaves and berries around neckline, filling in spaces as you go. Design will vary depending on size of sweatshirt. Cut one or two holly leaves from scraps to fill in holes (such as above knot on bow). Iron pieces as you are happy with the placement; be sure all edges are secured. Re-iron if necessary, but do not overheat (iron three to seven seconds only).

4 Rest tip of fabric paint bottle on appliqué/sweatshirt edge and outline leaves with green, berries with red, and bow with gold. All neckline pieces must be connected with paint to lock the sweatshirt when cut. If there are large empty spaces at neckline, small dots of gold can be added for filler and color. Add detail lines to center of holly and to bow (follow finished picture). Let dry 24 hours.

5 Cut neckline ribbing away, following the appliqué wreath. Cut line should be as close to paint line as possible, without cutting paint.

✱ See pages 117–123 for patterns

The blending of French horn, pine boughs, ribbons, and flowers will create musical memories!

• MATERIALS •

1 block dried floral foam

1-ounce package green moss

Craft pins

14-inch brass French horn

6 silver tinseled pine stems, 16 inches each

Wire cutters

6 green pine sprays, 16 inches each

3 yards red plaid ribbon, $2\frac{5}{8}$ inches wide

Wired wood picks

$3\frac{1}{2}$ yards metallic gold musical note ribbon, $1\frac{1}{4}$ inches wide

5 gold poinsettias, 3 inches each

2 holly berry sprays, 8 inches each

Chenille stem

Tacky glue

1 Cover foam block with moss and pin in place with craft pins.

3 Cut stems of two tinseled pine stems to a length of 12 inches. Insert one into each narrow end of floral foam. The pine should be placed under the horn.

2 Secure French horn to top edge of foam block with craft pins. You can also wire horn in place.

4 Cut green pine sprays into seven-inch pieces. Randomly insert these around foam, forming the outside shape of the wallpiece. Pine should outline shape of horn.

5 Cut a two-yard length of the plaid ribbon and form a four-loop bow with two five-inch loops, two seven-inch loops, and two six-inch streamers. Using wired pick, attach bow to pick and insert into center of design.

6 Cut four lengths of gold ribbon, each 24 inches long. Form four-loop bows with three-inch streamers and no center loop. Attach each to a wooden pick and insert into design around plaid bow. Fill in around bow loops with remaining tinseled pine stems.

7 Cut two 12-inch streamers from gold ribbon and a 12-inch streamer from plaid ribbon. Secure each to a wooden pick. Insert plaid streamer below plaid bow (on side of horn bell). Insert gold streamers to left of plaid streamer.

folded end. Insert two ends into back top of foam and glue. Push loop up for hanger.

8 Cut the stems of the poinsettias to a length of six inches. Insert them around design to fill space. Insert one holly berry spray above and one below plaid bow. Fold chenille stem in half and twist about two inches from

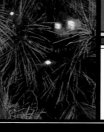

The tradition of hanging the stockings comes from long ago. Today, there is still excitement in this tradition on Christmas Eve, as families anticipate the goodies and presents from Santa. And the friendly snowman never looked better than when surrounded by glistening crystal stars!

• MATERIALS •

Red stocking

Transfer paper

Tracing paper

Pencil

Fabric paint: white, yellow, black, and glitter gold

Fabric brush

Fabric glue

10 emerald navette cabochons, 15 × 7mm

3 ruby faceted round stones, 7mm

13 dark sapphire faceted round stones, 7mm

7 emerald faceted round stones, 7mm

5 ruby faceted round stones, 9mm

17 crystal faceted round stones, 7mm

8 crystal faceted stars, 15mm

¼ yard satin ribbon, ⅛ inch wide

1 Adjust pattern size to fit your stocking. Trace pattern onto premade stocking. With black paint and fabric brush, paint hat (leave middle section red), mittens, and broom handle. Paint

Continued on next page

Continued from previous page

broom top and bottom yellow (leave middle section red). Paint snowman's body white. If one coat does not cover completely, apply more paint until the surface is evenly covered. Allow paint to dry (time may vary depending on type of paint used).

2 With glitter gold paint and fabric brush, lightly paint left side of hat, ribbon, scarf, and ground below snowman.

Outline all shapes and draw mouth with gold. Glue emerald navette cabochons and 7mm ruby faceted stones to hat. Place three 7mm dark sapphire faceted stones on face, two for eyes and one for the nose.

3 The remaining 7mm dark sapphires and emeralds will be used on scarf ends. To right scarf end, in last four sections, starting at top row, glue dark sapphire, emerald, dark sapphire. To second row, glue three dark sapphires. To third row, glue three emeralds. To fourth row, glue dark sapphire, emerald, dark sapphire. To left scarf end, at top row, glue dark sapphire, emerald, dark sapphire. To second row, glue emerald, dark sapphire. Glue 9mm rubies as buttons.

4 Randomly glue crystal and star stones around snowman. Make a bow with ribbon; glue to broom.

Giving warms our hearts and the hearts of those we love. The gift of a handmade basket can be enjoyed for many holiday seasons to come.

• MATERIALS •

White basket, medium size

1 stem glittered pine, with
    twelve 4-inch sections

Glue gun and glue sticks

1 yard red and green plaid
    ribbon, 1 inch wide

32-gauge cloth-covered
    wire

Wire cutters

1 stem gold glittered cedar
    spray, with six 4-inch
    sections

1 stem glittered white
    cedar, with eight 3-inch
    sections

1 shiny red berry spray,
    with 10 branches

4 gold jingle bells, $1\frac{1}{4}$
    inches each

1 Pull 12 sections off main stem of glittered pine. Glue these pieces in a loose L pattern along one side and up basket handle.

2 Make a four-loop bow with three-inch long loops. Secure with a two-inch length of cloth-covered wire. Set aside. Pull six sections off main stem of gold glittered cedar. Glue these to fill in pattern formed by pine pieces.

3 Pull eight sections off main stem of glittered white cedar. Glue these pieces evenly throughout design.

4 Cut berry spray into 10 sections. Place berries throughout design. Glue bow made in Step 2 into center bottom of design. Apply glue to each jingle bell and place evenly around bow.

"Santa Claus is comin' to town!" This folk art Santa is sure to bring a chuckle or two from young and old alike!

• MATERIALS •

4 × 4 inches wood post,
about 22 inches long

Handsaw

Pencil

Transparent paper

Tracing paper

Palette or palette paper

Acrylic Paints: fleshtone,
black, ivory, island coral,
berry red, liberty blue

¾-inch flat brush

10/0 detail brush

Spray satin sealer

Glue gun and glue sticks

15 to 20 strands raffia

2 silk holly leaves plus
berries

White pom-pon,
2 inches

1 Cut post to desired length. Trace pattern on page 61 using transparent paper and pencil. With tracing paper between transparent paper (carbon side down) and post, use a pencil to draw on lines for face and hat.

2 Use ¾-inch brush to paint face area with fleshtone paint. Paint hat with berry red. Paint hat fur, hair, mustache, and beard with ivory. Use one coat so that wood shows through, giving an aged appearance.

3 Use 10/0 brush to paint detail lines of hat, hair, and mustache in black. Paint iris of eyes liberty blue and pupils and eyelashes black. Add ivory eyebrows and highlight on lower right sides of eyes. Dip brush handle into ivory and dot the top of each eye. Add nose and lines around face with black. Using a dry brush, add a light coat of island coral to cheeks and tip of nose.

✱ Photocopy at 115%.

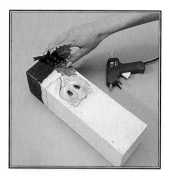

4 Spray post with satin sealer. Make a simple bow with raffia strands. Glue holly leaves and berries to top right side of hat. Glue raffia bow just above holly. Glue pom-pon to top of post.

• P A T E R N S •

Colorful lights are a part of our holiday decorating that expresses our joy and merriment in the season. This swag of painted wooden lights extends a warm welcome to all your visitors!

• MATERIALS •

7 bulbs cut from pine stock

Scroll or band saw

Power drill

Sandpaper or sanding pads

Acrylic paints: bright red,
    liberty blue*, Christmas
    green, pumpkin, white,
    black, luscious lemon,
    metallic gold

¾-inch flat brush

10/0 detail brush

Satin sealer

6 inches rattail cord

1 Cut seven bulbs from pine stock with scroll saw or band saw. Drill a ⅛-inch hole in top of each bulb. Lightly sand all bulbs.

2 Using ¾-inch flat
brush, paint two
bulbs bright red, two luscious lemon, one
Christmas green, one
pumpkin, and one liberty
blue.* Paint tops of each
bulb metallic gold. Let dry.

3 Use 10/0 detail
brush to add detail
lines to each bulb, includ-
ing letters. Use white paint
to make a comma stroke in
upper left of each bulb.
Brush on satin sealer.
Let dry.

*For photographic reasons,
we substituted a second
pumpkin bulb for the
liberty blue

*Photocopy pattern at 125 %.

4 String rattail cord through "W" bulb and tie a knot at top of bulb; leave a few inches of tail to left. Repeat with each bulb, leaving about two inches of cord between bulbs.

• P A T T E R N S •

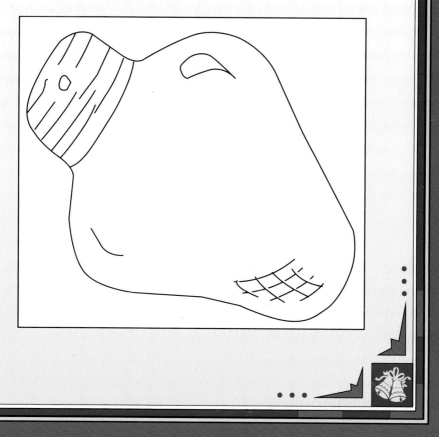

Poinsettias, the traditional Christmas flower, embellish this festive place setting. Would you believe a potato and some paint were all that was needed to achieve these results? Just cut a potato and watch your creativity bloom! Then to top your place setting off, make a napkin ring to complement your designs.

MATERIALS

White placemats

Napkins

Iron

4 large potatoes

Large knife

Sharp pencil

Craft knife

Fabric paints: yellow light, lacquer red, medium green, diamond yellow, sparkling ruby, lime

green, yellow

3 flat brushes, ¾ inch each

Palette or palette paper

Scratch paper for practice

6 inches red bendable ribbon for each ring, ¾ inch wide

Scissors

Glue gun and glue sticks

Silk holly sprigs with berries

1 Wash and dry placemats and napkins. Press. Use large knife to slice potatoes in half lengthwise for flowers and large leaf shapes; in half widthwise for small ones. Draw design on potato

Continued on next page

Continued from previous page

with pencil before carving with craft knife. Trim edges down. After you've carved a basic leaf shape, cut a center line with lines slanting upward on either side of center. Cut three to five leaf shapes, and two flowers. Carve several small circles in the center of each flower.

are lacquer red and sparkling ruby. Flower centers are yellow light and diamond yellow. Leaves are medium green and lime green. Do not dilute paints. Use a different brush for each color group.

3 Dry potatoes. Use a brush to apply paint, then press onto scratch paper. If you aren't happy, recut it or try again on a fresh potato.

2 Squeeze or scoop paints onto palette. Colors will be mixed as you apply them to carved potatoes. The poinsettias

5 Next, paint a large leaf: half with lime green, the other half with medium green. Add a few brush strokes of contrasting green on either side, in same direction as veins. Place leaf next to flower on placemat; press to transfer. Before repainting stamp, restamp to create a lighter background stamp that fills in white space around flower. Add more leaves of various sizes around flower.

4 Paint poinsettia. Place potato on a corner of placemat and press onto fabric; carefully lift up placemat and rub underside to help paint transfer. Lift potato; touch up areas that didn't print with a paintbrush.

6 After surrounding first poinsettia with leaves, add another red blossom and surround it with leaves. Work your way around placemat in this manner, always filling in leaves before printing another blossom. Alternate poinsettia stamps as you move around placemat, as well as turning them in different directions for variety. Do the same for leaves, especially when they fall side by side. Avoid symmetry. As you work, turn placemat around to see it from different angles.

7 To cover little holes of white, use a leaf stamp with little paint and lightly press on a spot to fill in with a background leaf. For edges, print a few leaves half on and half off placemat. Use yellow paint to add small raised dots in center of each poinsettia.

9 For napkin rings:
Hot glue ribbon
ends together.

8 To print napkin,
work as you did on
placemat. The paints used
on this project do not
require heat setting. Wait
48 hours before launder-
ing.

10 Glue holly sprig over
joint, pointing up.
Glue another sprig on top
of first, pointing in oppo-
site direction.

Apples and spice and everything nice are the ingredients for this tabletop arrangement. Festive plaid ribbon, bells, cinnamon sticks and delightful packages are nestled into the branches of the tree. What a very merry accent for a very Merry Christmas!

• MATERIALS •

Red bushel basket, about 9 inches around and 7 inches tall

Glue

Cloth-covered wire

$3\frac{1}{3}$ yards plaid ribbon, $1\frac{1}{2}$ inches wide

10 glittered plastic pine sprigs, 3 inches long each

16 assorted Christmas packages, about $1\frac{1}{2}$ inches each

Novelty Santa

2 yards green satin ribbon, $\frac{1}{8}$ inch wide

7 gold jingle bells, $\frac{7}{8}$ inch each

$2\frac{2}{3}$ yards red satin ribbon, $\frac{1}{8}$ inch wide

36 cinnamon sticks, $2\frac{1}{2}$ inches long

18 red lacquered apples, $\frac{7}{8}$ inch wide

Tabletop Christmas tree, 24 inches tall

18 ornaments with bow and two jingle bells, $\frac{3}{4}$ inch

1 Cut a two-yard length of plaid ribbon and secure with wire. Make an eight-loop bow, each loop measuring three inches with 12-inch streamers. Glue bow to top edge of basket. Drape streamers about two inches from bottom of basket and secure with glue.

2 Glue glittered pine sprigs around top edge of basket. Slightly overlap sprigs.

3 Glue a package in middle of bow and the rest around top edge of basket. Glue Santa to basket edge, just right of bow.

4 Cut one 6-inch length, five 8-inch lengths, and one 10-inch length of green ribbon. Tie a jingle bell to each length of ribbon by looping ribbon through hole in top of bell, bringing ends together and tying.

5 Glue three bells in a cluster under center bow on basket. Glue the other four equally spaced around outside of basket.

6 To decorate the tree: Form ornaments by gluing three cinnamon sticks together. Cut 12 eight-inch lengths of red ribbon. Glue middle of ribbon onto cluster of cinnamon sticks. Bring ribbon ends together and tie a knot.

8 Form an eight-loop bow with remaining plaid ribbon. Each loop should measure 2½ inches. Attach to top of tree. Insert decorated tree into basket.

7 Glue red apples, bell and bow ornaments, and cinnamon stick ornaments to tree branches.

MATERIALS

⅓ sheet plastic canvas, #7
   mesh

#16 tapestry needle

Worsted weight yarn:
   White, 20 yards
   Red, 5 yards
   Green, 4 yards
   Yellow, 1 yard

4 acrylic coasters

Instructions:

Cut four pieces of canvas 19 holes × 19 holes. Trim according to dark outer lines of charts.

Stitch pieces following charts, noting that most is worked in continental stitch. The green portions of large package are cross-

Continued on next page

Protect your tables and decorate your home with these fun and easy plastic canvas coasters. Stitched in no time, you can make them for your home and give them as gifts to special friends!

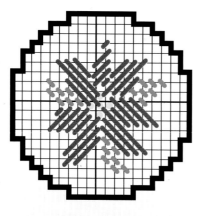

Continued from previous page

stitched. Back-stitch bows
on wreath, bell, and large
gift. Work holly berries,
poinsettia center, clapper
on bell, and knots on bows
in French knots. Work
poinsettia in long straight
stitches, noting direction of
stitches. Overcast all edges
in white.

Before mounting coast-
ers, discard foam inserts.
Peel adhesive backing from
a styrene piece from coaster, and lay finished coaster
on top, centering carefully.
Insert into an acrylic coaster, pressing to secure.
Repeat with other three
coasters.

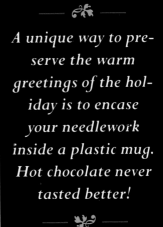

• MATERIALS •

2 red mugs (with vinyl
    weave inserts)

#24 tapestry needle

Floss: red, green

Scissors

Instructions:

Cross-stitch with three of six strands of floss. Take mug apart and remove vinyl weave strip. Find center horizontally and vertically and mark with a pin or needle. Find center of chart by using arrows to determine where to begin stitching.

For second mug, insert Joy in place of Noel. When stitching is completed, insert vinyl weave back into mug, placing seams next to handle area. Snap insert back into mug.

• P A T T E R N S •

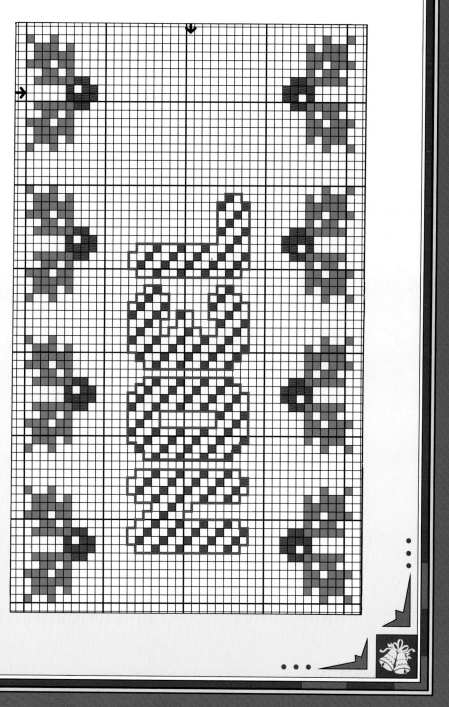

Sheer white ribbon woven through pine boughs, gold pinecones, and glittering snowflakes reminds us of the beauty of a picture-perfect white Christmas—even on the warmest holiday morning!

MATERIALS

20 pinecones, 2 inches each

Gold metallic spray

Glue gun and glue

Pine wreath, 20 inches wide

5 yards white / gold sheer
   wired ribbon with gold
   stars, 3 inches wide

Scissors

Cloth-covered wire

Wire cutters

10 plastic frosted
   snowflakes, 4 inches each

$2\frac{1}{3}$ yards of gold metallic
   tubing, $\frac{3}{8}$ inch wide

1 Spray pinecones
with gold spray.
Allow to dry. Apply
glue to each pinecone
and position throughout
wreath.

3 Drape remaining ribbon around wreath, using wired pine branches to wrap around ribbon and hold in place.

2 Form an eight-loop bow with the sheer wired ribbon. Each loop should measure 3½ inches. Cut off remaining ribbon. Secure bow with cloth-covered wire. Wire the bow onto the wreath, securing with extra wire.

4 Apply a small amount of glue to one tip of each snowflake and place around wreath.

5 Cut metallic tubing into 12-inch lengths. Form two loops with each length and secure with cloth-covered wire. Trim excess wire. Glue these throughout design.

A luscious wreath filled with sugarplums for all the good little girls and boys, young and old, to enjoy. Confections are one of the delights of the Christmas season—they can be decorative and delicious!

Creative Candy Wreath

• MATERIALS •

1-inch straight pins

Tacky glue

Plastic foam wreath, 12 inches around

9 yards Christmas ribbon, 2½ inches wide

Stapler and staples

Cloth-covered wire

8 yards each red, green, silver, and gold metallic curling ribbon, ¼ inch wide

Red peppermint candies

1 Dip all pins into glue before inserting into wreath. Secure one end of Christmas ribbon to back of foam wreath with a few straight pins. Tightly wrap wreath with ribbon to completely cover. Trim away excess ribbon.

2 Use remainder of
Christmas ribbon
and form box pleats
around outside back of
wreath. Staple pleats to
hold. Pin pleats in place
around wreath back.

3 Secure candy to
wreath with straight
pins dipped in glue. (If you
wish people to eat the
candy, don't dip pins into
glue.) Equally space candy
along wreath.

4 Cut six 1-yard lengths each of red, green, silver, and gold curling ribbons. Form each length into a six-loop bow with loops measuring $1\frac{1}{2}$ inches, securing with wire. Secure each to wreath with pins. Use the bows to fill in space around candy.

5 Cut remaining curling ribbon into 6-inch lengths, curl and tie onto ends of candies randomly throughout design.

The delicate pattern of snowflakes will generate a blizzard of compliments! Once you've cut out the snowflakes, you can make many different versions— think of all the possibilities.

• M A T E R I A L S •

12 to 15 squares of paper,
  about 4½ square inches

Scissors

Iron

White paper

Plastic snowflakes
  (optional)

Blue spray paint

1 Start with a square
of paper. Fold bot-
tom edge of square up to
top edge to make a rectangle. Fold this rectangle in
half so you have a square.
Fold this square from corner to corner to create a
triangle.

3 Now you're ready to cut designs in the paper with the scissors. Some designs can be cut on the side with the single fold, but don't cut it away completely or snowflake will fall apart. Experiment with cutting out diamonds, circles, and odd shapes from the multicreased side. Unfold paper. Cut 12 to 15 snowflakes. Iron them so they lie flat. Iron sheets of white paper.

2 With the single fold at the bottom, fold side with several creases to touch bottom edge. Cut off the paper hanging off the end of the fold.

5 Shake can of paint well before spraying lightly over paper, using a gentle back and forth motion. Hold can high off paper, and spray directly above to avoid moving snowflakes. Allow to dry for a few minutes so you don't smudge paint when you remove snowflakes. Snowflakes can be reused.

4 In a well-ventilated area, arrange snowflakes on white paper so they overlap slightly. If you have plastic snowflakes, use them to weigh down paper ones.

Sweet confections border a tree skirt. Gingerbread boys, candy canes, and holly leaves are ironed on—a perfect complement to a lovely Christmas tree!

MATERIALS

1 yard red felt

Chalk

String

Iron

1 yard fusible webbing

¼ yard washable green satin

⅓ yard brown imitation suede

¼ yard mini-print Christmas fabric

Scissors

Fabric paints: copper glitter, green shiny, pearl, red shiny, black shiny

Fabric glitter: medium, fine

1 yard Christmas ribbon

3 safety pins

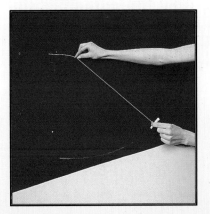

1 Chalk a 34-inch circle on felt material.

2 Iron adhesive to back of material. On medium setting, place iron on paper side of adhesive and press for three to five seconds. Trace patterns on paper back of prepared materials. Use green for 17 holly leaves. Use brown for eight small and six large gingerbread boys. Use mini-print for 15 candy canes. Cut out and peel paper off pieces.

3 Position gingerbread, holly, and candy canes around chalk edge. Place three candy canes between center and border. Iron appliqués to felt, let cool. Be sure all edges are secured. Re-iron if necessary, but do not overheat (iron three to seven seconds only).

✱See pages 127–128 for patterns

4 Rest tip of fabric paint bottle on appliqué/felt edge and outline each piece. Outline holly with green, gingerbread with copper glitter, and candy cane with pearl.

Add detail lines to center of holly and stripe on candy canes. Dry-brush gingerbread cheeks red and add facial features in black. Finish icing detail with pearl, buttons and bows with red and green (follow picture). Use pearl paint to add curly stems and dots to fill in noticeable spaces in border. Sprinkle glitter (medium and fine) over wet fabric paint.

line should be close to paint, but should not cut into it.

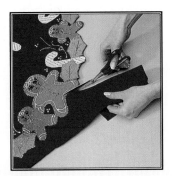

6 Draw and cut a line from center to rear break on border design. Cut out a 2½-inch circle in center for tree. Make bows for center candy canes and safety pin from underneath.

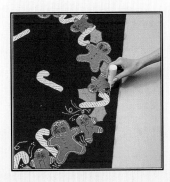

5 Let dry, then shake off excess glitter. Cut away excess felt, leaving a scalloped edge. Cut

Every year we like to add new ornaments to our Christmas tree collection. Beautifully stitched ornaments, such as these cross-stitch ones, are especially appealing!

• MATERIALS •

1 yard white cross-stitch cloth, #14 count

#24 tapestry needle

Floss: yellow, orange, pink, red, burgundy, emerald, forest, purple, ivory, light tan, black, dark red, tan, brown

Scissors

Glue gun and glue sticks

Adhesive-backed mounting board

4 yards red gathered ribbon

1 yard red satin ribbon, ⅛ inch wide

1 square green felt (optional)

Instructions:

Stitch according to printed charts and instructions. To finish: Trim cross-stitching to desired shapes and sizes. Cut pieces of adhesive-backed mounting board to match shapes. Affix cross-stitching to mounting board backings. Using a glue gun or thick white craft glue, starting at the bottom center of each design, carefully glue the ribbon around the outside edge of each design, slightly overlapping at the bottom. Make a loop from eight inches red satin ribbon, and glue to top back side of each piece for a hanger. If desired, cut pieces of green felt to cover backs of ornaments, gluing them in place.

· PATTERNS ·

Yellow
Orange
Pink
Red
Burgundy
Emerald
Forest
Purple
Ivory
Light Tan
Black
Dark Red
Tan
Brown

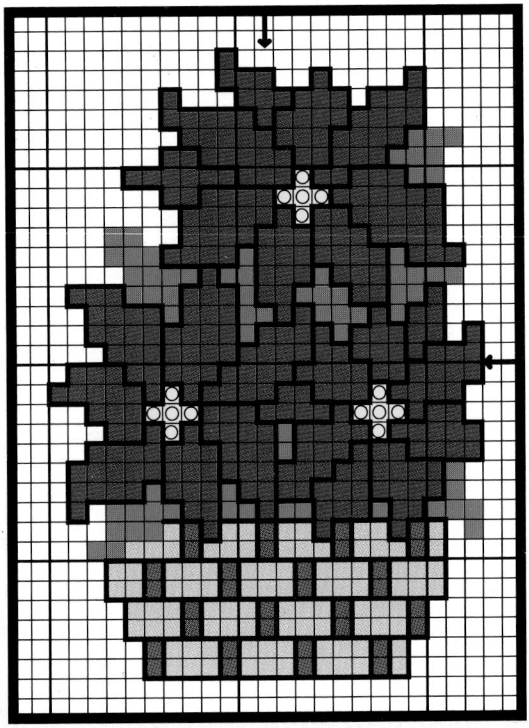

Clay ornaments can be a fun family project—and easy enough for a child. Once Mom or Dad bakes them, they'll last forever!

• MATERIALS •

Waxed paper

Polymer clay: 2 packages
    brown, 1 red, 1 white, 2
    green, 2 bronze, 1 yellow

Transparent paper

Pencil

Rolling pin

Craft knife

Paper clips (for hangers)

Wire cutters

Cookie sheet (nonconduct-
    ing surface)

Metal spatula

Brown paper bags

Paintbrush

Varnish (for modeling com-
    pounds)

Red and white ribbon, $\frac{1}{8}$
    inch wide (optional)

1 For holly ornament:
Twine green and
bronze coils together and
fold them back on them-
selves, twisting the new
coil until you have a mar-
bled pattern.

General information: Cover your work surface with waxed paper. Work with the lightest color first; darker colors stain. Work the clay in your hands to soften it, then roll it into a coil. Use the same method with the other color.

2 Roll coil flat. When it's ¼ to ⅛ inch thick, use holly pattern and craft knife to make two leaves. Lightly score surfaces. Press leaf on tops together.

3 From red coil, pull off three small pieces for berries. Roll them into pea-sized balls. Push berries gently onto tops of leaves.

4 To make a metal hanger for holly and gingerbread man, partially unbend a paper clip and cut off all but ½-inch loop. Poke this into the top of ornament.

5 Bake on a noncon- ducting surface (slate or Pyrex®) in a 250 degree oven for 15 to 30 minutes. Clay will be soft when hot, it hardens as it cools. Ventilate kitchen when baking. Do not over

bake; fumes could be toxic. Remove ornaments with spatula and place on brown paper bag. (Keep cookie sheet utensils for clay only!) Once the ornament is cool, brush on varnish. Glue a ribbon on candy canes for hangers and a bow to holly.

2 Gently roll colors together to form one large roll. Roll should be about ½ inch thick. Trim ends and twist so colors spiral. Bend head to form candy cane shape (Go to Step 5).

1 For candy cane: See general information. Roll out the coils until long and thin. Cut white coil in half, then cut red coils to same length. Layer white and red, then red and white on top.

1 For gingerbread man: See general information. Use rolling pin to flatten brown clay to ¼ inch thick. Make a gingerbread man using pattern on page 126; cut around edges with craft knife.

2 Roll bits of yellow, red, and green clay into small balls (pea sized) for buttons. Roll two small white balls for eyes, flatten slightly. Press a bit of green into middle of white. Roll out small pieces of yellow, red, and green for rickrack. With a craft knife, cut a zigzag pattern and place on arms, legs, and neck. Roll a thin red tube for mouth (Go to Step 4).

• PATTERNS •

Stitched Accessories

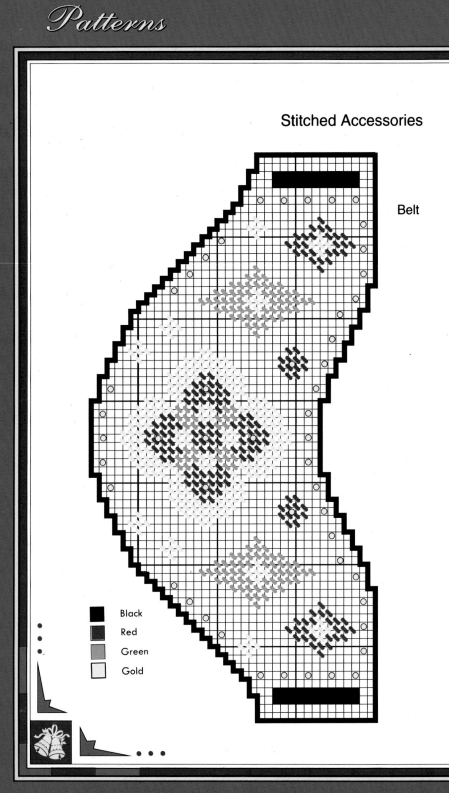

Belt

Black
Red
Green
Gold

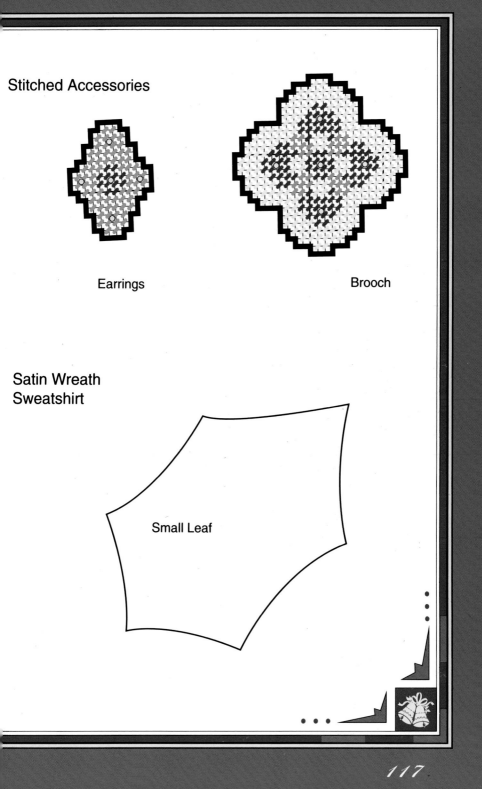

Stitched Accessories

Earrings

Brooch

Satin Wreath Sweatshirt

Small Leaf

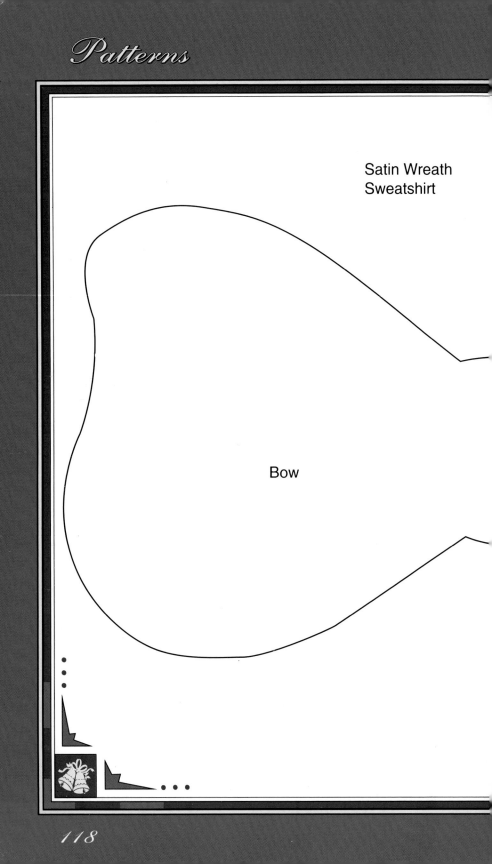

Satin Wreath
Sweatshirt

Bow

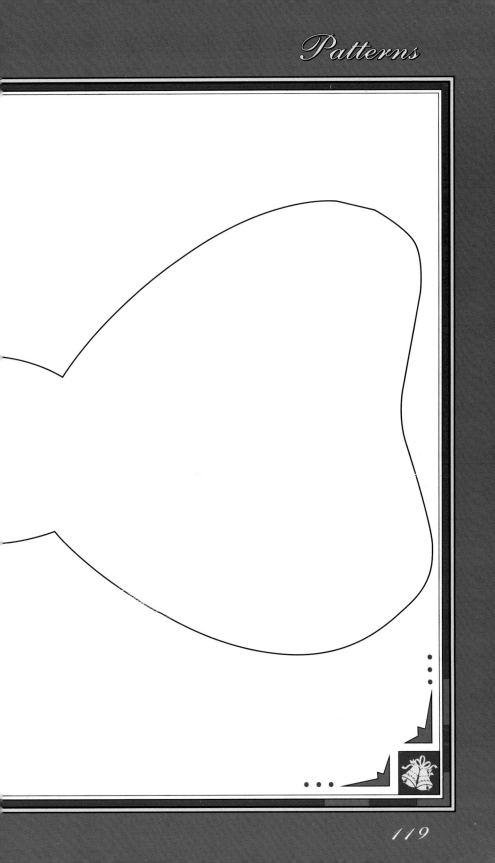

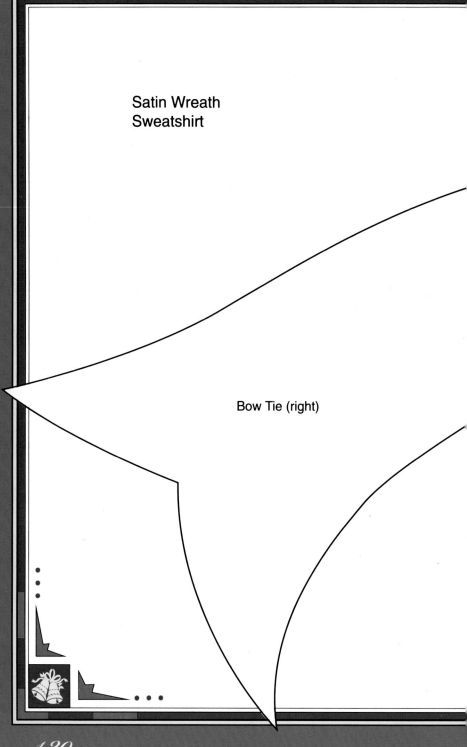

Satin Wreath
Sweatshirt

Bow Tie (right)

Bow Knot

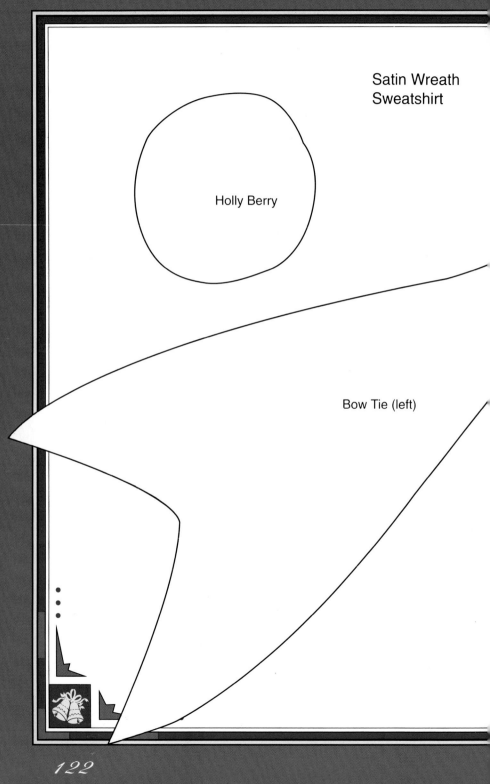

Satin Wreath
Sweatshirt

Holly Berry

Bow Tie (left)

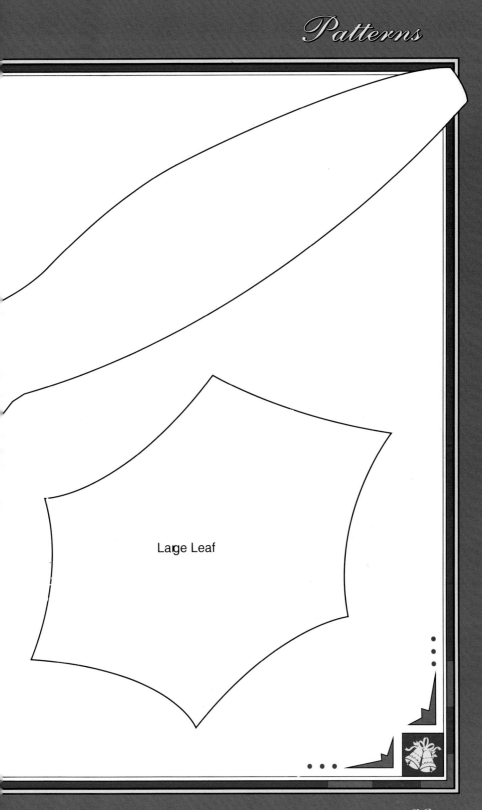

Large Leaf

Snowman
Stocking

Family Fun
Project

Snowman
Stocking

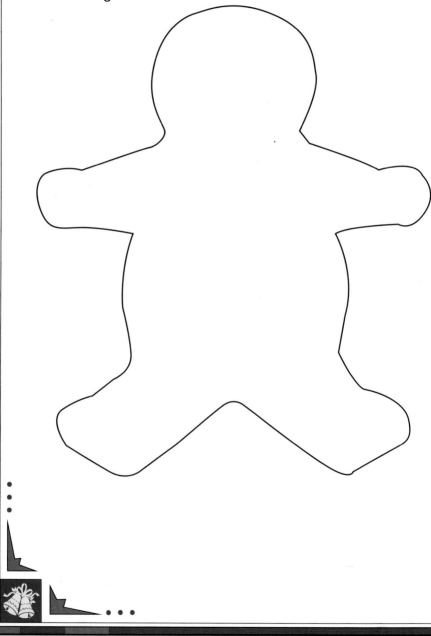

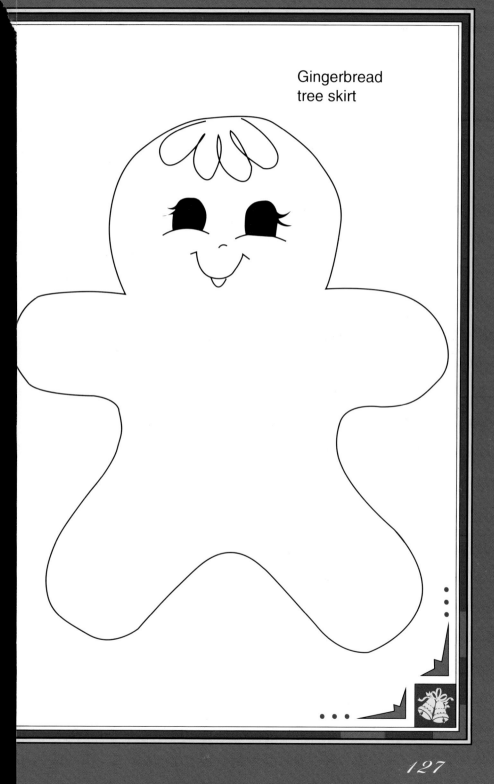

Gingerbread
tree skirt

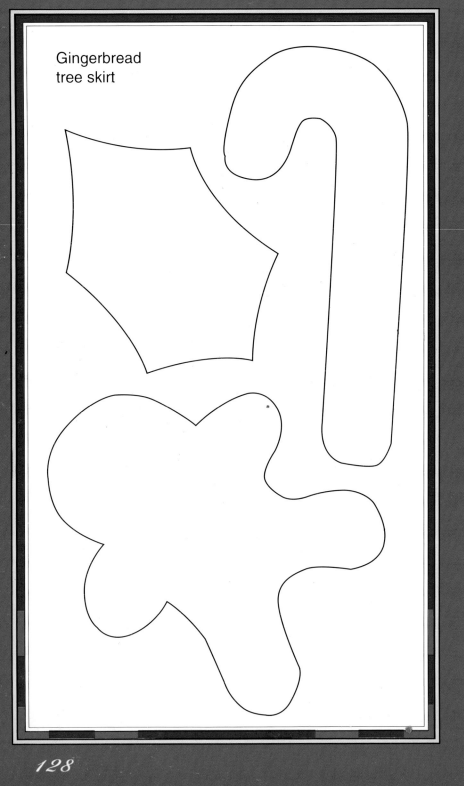

Gingerbread
tree skirt